Dominoes

THE CURSE
OF THE
MUMMY

OXFORD

OXFORD

UNIVERSITY PRESS

Great Clarendon Street, Oxford OX2 6DP

Oxford University Press is a department of the University of Oxford.
It furthers the University's objective of excellence in research, scholarship,
and education by publishing worldwide in

Oxford New York

Auckland Cape Town Dar es Salaam Hong Kong Karachi
Kuala Lumpur Madrid Melbourne Mexico City Nairobi
New Delhi Shanghai Taipei Toronto

With offices in

Argentina Austria Brazil Chile Czech Republic France Greece
Guatemala Hungary Italy Japan Poland Portugal Singapore
South Korea Switzerland Thailand Turkey Ukraine Vietnam

OXFORD and OXFORD ENGLISH are registered trade marks of
Oxford University Press in the UK and in certain other countries

ISBN: 978 0 19 424342 1

A complete recording of this Dominoes edition of *The Curse of the Mummy*
is available on cassette ISBN 978 0 19 424358 2

Printed in China

ACKNOWLEDGEMENTS

The publisher would like to thank the following for permission to reproduce photographs: Ancient
Egypt Picture Library pp iv (eggs in bowl), 19 (Hathor), 42 (board game, silver wine jar,
basket of dates, chair); Robert Harding Picture Library pp iv (gold coffin/F.L. Kenett &
G Rianbird Ltd, Anubis, guard statue), 25 (winged scarab), 30 (guard statue), 39 (gold
openwork), 42 (head rest, earrings); Mark Mason Studios p 43 (all objects); Werner
Forman Archive p 24 (Anubis/E. Stronhal), 31 (Sphinx at Giza).

Dominoes

SERIES EDITORS: BILL BOWLER AND SUE PARMINTER

THE CURSE
OF THE
MUMMY

JOYCE HANNAM

Illustrated by Jocelyn Gicquel

LEVEL ONE ■ 400 HEADWORDS

Joyce Hannam has taught English in several European countries including Greece, Spain, Turkey and the Czech Republic. She now lives in York, in the north of England, and works mainly with Japanese university students and business people from Germany, Italy, France and Spain. She has written a number of other stories for students of English, including *The Death of Karen Silkwood* in the Oxford Bookworms Library.

OXFORD

BEFORE READING

1 Look at the plan of Tutankhamun's tomb when Howard Carter found it. Match the pictures with the rooms on the plan.

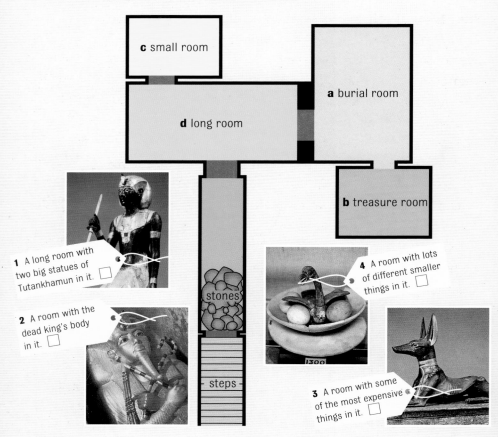

c small room

a burial room

d long room

b treasure room

1 A long room with two big statues of Tutankhamun in it. ☐

2 A room with the dead king's body in it. ☐

stones

4 A room with lots of different smaller things in it. ☐

steps

3 A room with some of the most expensive things in it. ☐

2 When did Carter go into the different rooms? What do you think? Put them in order. Number them 1–4.

a ☐ burial room

b ☐ treasure room

c ☐ small room

d ☐ long room

Chapter 1

Where are Tutankhamun's treasures?

August 4th 1922: The Valley of the Kings
Here I am at last in the **Valley** of the **Kings**! It's a valley in the **desert** with lots of **sand** and the **tombs** of dead Egyptian kings in it. It took us a long time to get here, and we all felt very hot when we arrived, but that doesn't matter now. It's good to be here.

I'm happy to be working with Mr Carter. Lots of young men wanted to work with him in the Valley of the Kings, but he took me because of my father. My father and Mr Carter are good friends. They often meet at the **museum** in Cairo. My father works there. Also, I'm a good **artist**. And I know a lot about **Tutankhamun**, too. Did you know he was a king when he was only nine years old? But he wasn't king for very long. He died when he was eighteen. That's only one year older than me! Why did he die then? Perhaps we can find the answer when we find his tomb. Mr Carter thinks it's in the Valley of the Kings. He began looking for it five years ago, and he doesn't want to

valley land between two hills

king the most important man in a country

desert a place which has no water

sand it is yellow and we find a lot of it in the desert

tomb where people put a dead person

museum a building with old things in it

artist a person who makes pictures

Tutankhamun /tuːtənkɑːˈmuːn/

stop. Some people think he's **crazy**, but I don't. Nearly all the other old Egyptian kings have a tomb here, so why not Tutankhamun?

There are about twenty of us, men and boys, working here in the valley. Perhaps I can make friends later, but for now I'm going to write this **diary** and my diary can be my friend. There aren't any shops or cinemas here, so I need something to do in the evenings. And perhaps one day people are going to want to read my diary. Why? Well, perhaps we're going to find Tutankhamun's tomb, or a different king's tomb, or some new **treasures**. Egyptian tombs have lots of treasures in them, you know – **gold** and **jewels**. But **thieves** took treasures from many of the tombs in the past. And there are tomb thieves in Egypt today, too. People come from all over the world to look for gold and jewels. When they find a tomb, they take all the treasure home to their countries. I think that's very bad. I'm happy to say Mr Carter is not a thief. He says Egyptian treasures must stay in Egypt. I think he's right.

But our work's not going to be easy. Mr Carter has only one year now to find Tutankhamun's tomb. He's got a rich friend, **Lord** Carnarvon, and he gives Mr Carter money to help with our work. Lord Carnarvon likes Egypt a lot and he loves old Egyptian treasures. He's got lots of them in his home in England. But after giving Mr Carter money for five years he must be careful. Not long ago he called Mr Carter to England and told him, 'Only one more year looking for Tutankhamun, Howard.' Mr Carter came back to Egypt at once. He brought a little yellow **bird** with him.

'That bird is going to help us find Tutankhamun's tomb,' said Karim. He's one of the boys working in the valley with me. How can a little bird help us? I don't know. But it's

crazy not thinking well

diary a book where you write about what happens every day

treasure something expensive, like gold or jewels

gold an expensive yellow metal

jewel an expensive stone

thief (*plural* **thieves**) a person who takes things without asking

lord an important, rich man

bird an animal that can fly through the sky

true we need some help – from something or someone.

Perhaps you think a year's a long time? It's not when you're looking for a little tomb in a very big valley. Where are all of Tutankhamun's treasures? Mr Carter thinks he knows – and I think he's right, but let's wait and see!

Well, good night, diary – from me, Tariq.

Good night, diary.

August 25th 1922

Today I'm going to tell you something about our days in the desert. We begin work very early every morning when the sun comes up. We **dig** for six hours with not much water to drink. At twelve o'clock, it is very, very hot. So we stop to eat, to drink, and to sleep. After two hours we begin digging again. We stop when it gets dark. My back and my arms always feel bad in the evenings. We're very hungry when the sun goes down and the nights in the desert are very cold. Everyone is tired, so we don't talk much when we're eating dinner.

I don't know what other people think about all day, but I think about Tutankhamun. Mr Carter says he lived with his brothers and sisters when he was a little boy. Later he **married** the beautiful **Ankhesenamun**. Some people say he has no tomb because he died suddenly when he was very young. But tombs were very important in old Egypt and Mr Carter thinks Tutankhamun has his tomb somewhere in this valley. But where?

dig (*past* **dug**) to take away sand or earth

marry to make someone your husband or wife

Ankhesenamun /ˌæŋkəˈsenəmən/

It's late now and the sky is dark. Suddenly I feel cold. Is Tutankhamun's body in a tomb somewhere near us now? Are we going to find it soon? Is Mr Carter's little yellow bird going to help us or not? Who knows?

September 12th 1922

Some visitors came to the Valley of the Kings today. People often come here to look at the open tombs. They look at the pictures in the tombs and the bodies of the dead kings – we call them **mummies**, you know. Today's visitors were artists from France. They said everyone in Europe is interested in Egypt now. They are building new 'Egyptian' cinemas and hotels in the big cities. And shops are selling 'Egyptian' beds, tables, chairs, and pictures too. Artists can make a lot of money with Egyptian things. A young girl with dark hair and a beautiful, strong face walked along the valley behind the other artists. For a minute, she looked at me. Then suddenly she dropped something in the sand and began to look for it. I went to help her. After a minute, I found it – a gold **bracelet** with an Egyptian eye on it. I gave it to her and she smiled.

'Thank you,' she said. 'My teacher, Mr Ayrton, gave it to me for my birthday. Isn't it nice? I didn't want to lose it.'

She had beautiful dark eyes. I wanted to speak to her, but what could I say? *'Excuse me, Anne, you have a beautiful face.'* Of course not!

I know her name is Anne because an older man called to her 'Come on, Anne!'

'Coming, Mr Ayrton,' she said, and she ran after him.

In the evening, the French artists left and went back to their hotel in Luxor. Anne smiled at me when she left, but then her teacher, Mr Ayrton, called her and the smile left

mummy the dead body of an Egyptian king

bracelet a ring that you wear on your arm

4

her face and she ran after him again.

Am I going to see Anne again? I like her a lot, but I don't like her teacher, Mr Ayrton. He's a lot older than her. Perhaps he's a very good artist, but why must she run to him every time he calls her? She needs to be with young people, not old Mr Ayrton!

It's another beautiful night tonight. Desert nights are wonderful. But again I feel very cold. I think the dead kings come near us and watch us at night. I can feel their dead eyes looking at us coldly. Some people think they're angry with us for digging here. They say bad things happen to people when they go into Egyptian tombs looking for treasure. But Mr Carter is OK, and he began digging in Egypt years ago. So perhaps they're wrong!

I gave it to her and she smiled.

READING CHECK

Are these sentences true or false? Tick the boxes.

		True	False
a	Howard Carter is telling the story.	☐	☑
b	Tariq is helping Mr Carter look for Tutankhamun's tomb.	☐	☐
c	Lord Carnarvon is giving money to Mr Carter.	☐	☐
d	Tutankhamun died when he was very old.	☐	☐
e	Some Italian artists came to visit on September 12th 1922.	☐	☐
f	One of the artists, Anne, has an older teacher, Mr Ayrton.	☐	☐
g	Tariq likes Mr Ayrton.	☐	☐

WORD WORK

1 Match the words with the pictures.

1 valley **2** marry **3** gold **4** diary **5** jewel

6 desert **7** king **8** thief **9** bracelet

2 Write the words to match the things in the picture.

artist   bird   dig   ~~mummy~~   sand   tomb   treasure

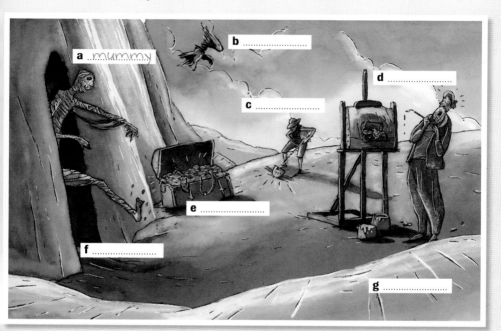

a .....mummy.....
b ....
c ....
d ....
e ....
f ....
g ....

GUESS WHAT

What happens in the next chapter? Tick four boxes.

a ☐ Mr Carter's men find the door to a tomb in the sand.
b ☐ Mr Carter wants to tell everyone all about his work.
c ☐ Mr Carter's yellow bird dies.
d ☐ A mummy begins to kill people.
e ☐ Lord Carnarvon comes to Egypt with his daughter.
f ☐ Carnarvon and Carter are excited when they look at the tomb door.

Chapter 2

There's something here!

November 4th 1922

step a part of
a stair

voice you use
this to speak

Something wonderful happened today! We found a **step** in the sand. It was about 4 p.m. when someone suddenly cried out behind me. It was my friend Karim.

'Tariq, quick, there's something here!' I ran to him and we dug fast. We soon found a step in the sand and under the first step we could see a second one.

I said 'Stop! We must get Mr Carter.' Someone found Mr Carter and he ran over to us. When he saw the step, he was very excited and he couldn't speak. We all waited. Then he found his **voice**. 'Dig' he cried. 'Dig I say!' So we all dug very quickly and we found five more steps before the sun went down. Then we stopped.

Now we are all very tired, but very excited. At dinner there were many questions in all our heads: 'What are we going to find next?' 'Is there a tomb here?' 'Is it going to be open or closed?'

We soon found a step in the sand.

Early tomorrow morning we must dig more. I don't think I'm going to sleep very much tonight. At last there is something new in the sand. And my friend Karim found it!

November 6th 1922

Tonight I can tell my diary everything. But only my diary. Mr Carter says we can't tell people about the steps in the sand. He says they're very important.

Today we found sixteen steps in the sand. Then we found a door. And the most important thing – the door wasn't open, but had old Egyptian **seals** on it. Mr Carter went down the steps and looked at the seals very carefully for a long time. We all waited in the sand under the hot sun. Down in the dark, looking at that old Egyptian door, Mr Carter began to laugh.

'They're his seals,' he called up to us. 'Tutankhamun's seals! I think it's his tomb at last! Well done everybody!'

We all laughed and cried. It was very exciting! But after a time, Mr Carter said we must all be quiet. He doesn't want **newspaper** men to hear about this and to come to the Valley of the Kings bringing lots of visitors.

'First, I must tell Lord Carnarvon,' said Mr Carter. 'We can't open the door without him. Put all the sand back and say nothing about this.'

So we **covered** the door and all the steps under the sand again. And now we must wait for Lord Carnarvon. It's going to take two weeks or more for him to come to Egypt by ship from England. How can we keep quiet for two weeks? It's a good thing I'm far from my family. And that beautiful French artist Anne is far away now. I think she would like to hear all about this, too. Without them here, there's nobody to talk to – nobody but you, my diary.

seal something on a door which someone must break to open the door

newspaper people read about things that happen every day in this

cover to put something on so you can't see it

November 12th 1922

Something very **strange** happened today. A **snake** killed Mr Carter's yellow bird and ate it. Karim was ill, and his face went white, when he heard about it.

'The yellow bird helped us to find Tutankhamun's tomb,' he said, 'but now Tutankhamun sends this snake to kill the bird because he is angry with us. We must stop digging at once and never, never open the boy-king's tomb.'

Mr Carter told Karim to be quiet and not to say all those crazy things in front of the younger boys. 'Listen to me, Karim,' he said, 'Tutankhamun died thousands of years ago. He can't be angry with us, do you hear?'

Who is right about Tutankhamun? Mr Carter, or Karim? I don't know. But I'm beginning to feel afraid.

November 23rd 1922

Today at last Lord Carnarvon and his daughter, Evelyn, arrived. Lord Carnarvon doesn't look well. His face is very white and tired.

When they arrived, we took the sand off the steps and the door again. Lord Carnarvon and Mr Carter went down the steps to look at the seals on the door. They were very excited. Lord Carnarvon's daughter stood next to me on the first step and I heard her say: 'I **hope** there's something there this time. Oh, Father, you're very tired and ill! I hope this visit doesn't make you feel worse.'

She spoke very quietly, but I heard her.

Lord Carnarvon and Mr Carter stayed down looking at the door for a long time. They were very quiet. We went away to have something to eat and drink. When we came back an hour later, they came up the steps to meet us.

strange not usual

snake a long animal with no legs

hope to want something to be true

'Some of the seals on the door are **broken**,' said Lord Carnarvon. 'So we're not the first people to find the door. Perhaps the tomb behind the door has nothing in it.'

Nobody spoke. Everybody thought of all the gold and treasures we hoped to find there.

'But,' Lord Carnarvon continued, 'it's a wonderful thing to find a new tomb. We may find pictures on the **walls** or mummies or other beautiful things. Our work is very important. There are stones behind the door, and we must now move away the stones.'

So we worked all afternoon. The stones are big and heavy and I don't know when we're going to finish — perhaps tomorrow.

It is cold again tonight. Are we going to find treasure in Tutankhamun's tomb? Is his angry **spirit** near us, watching us? I am too tired to think or to write any more now. Good night, diary.

Lord Carnarvon and Mr Carter looked at the seals.

broken in pieces

wall the sides of a room; a room usually has four of these

spirit the part of a person that is not the body; some people think that it leaves the body when a person dies

11

READING CHECK

Complete the sentences with the correct names.

Tariq

Mr Carter

Karim

Lord Carnarvon

a ..Karim.... finds the first step in the sand.

b .... knows the door in the sand is to Tutankhamun's tomb.

c .... tells Lord Carnarvon about the door in the sand.

d .... thinks Tutankhamun is angry because people are opening his tomb.

e .... says Tutankhamun can't be angry because he died thousands of years ago.

f .... looks ill when he comes to see the door in the sand.

g .... hears Evelyn talking quietly to her father.

WORD WORK

1 Find the words in the stones to complete the sentences.

a 'Which n e w s p a p e r do you read every day?'
'Oh, *The Times*, of course.'

b 'What's the time?'
'I don't know. My watch is b _ _ _ _ _!'

c 'Look! Dad's asleep on the sand.'
'But it's cold! Let's c _ _ _ _ him with something!'

d 'What's that long black thing in the road?'
'I think it's a s _ _ _ _.'

e 'Does Tariq think Tutankhamun's s _ _ _ _ _ _ is angry with them?'
'He doesn't know.'

2 **Use the words in the steps to complete Evelyn's letter.**

hope

strange

steps

walls

seals

Mother,

Here we are in Egypt. Father and I are very tired. It's **(a)** .....strange... for us to be here after all that time on the ship. Daddy wanted to go down the **(b)** .... and see the door to the tomb when we arrived. There were **(c)** .... of an Egyptian King on it. I **(d)** .... we find something in the tomb and not only four **(e)** .... and no treasure!

love

Evelyn

GUESS WHAT

What happens in the next chapter? Match the first and the second parts of these sentences.

a Tariq thinks he sees . . .
b Carter's men find . . .
c Carter, Carnarvon and Tariq look at . . .
d Carter, Carnarvon, Evelyn and Tariq go into . . .
e Evelyn and Tariq are afraid of . . .
f Carter and Carnarvon leave . . .

g a second door to the tomb.
h Anne one night.
i the spirit of Tutankhamun.
j the tomb with lights one night.
k the tomb last of all.
l the things through a hole in the door.

Chapter 3

Into the tomb

November 26th 1922

It was late at night. I saw that French artist Anne far away in the desert. I felt happy. She came nearer and nearer to me. Now I could see her face and it was very **sad**. I wanted to speak to her, to take her in my arms, but she was far, far

sad not happy

away from me. Then I saw something moving in the sand next to her feet. It was a head and an arm. At first I thought it was old Mr Ayrton, her teacher, but then I saw it was the mummy of an old Egyptian king. Worse than that, it was alive!

'Anne!' I cried, and I ran to help her.

Then the mummy came out of the sand. It took Anne in its black arms and down they went into the sand.

Anne cried 'Help me, Tariq!' but there was nothing I could do.

There was nothing I could do.

I **woke up** in my bed in our **camp** feeling cold and afraid. It was only a **dream** after all!

We moved the last big stone at 5 p.m. today and we saw a second door behind the first! There were seals on this door too, and Mr Carter said they were Tutankhamun's seals again. But this time the seals were not broken. I could see Lord Carnarvon and Mr Carter were happy. But they didn't want to look excited in front of us.

'It's late,' they said to us. 'Of course we can't open the tomb without the most important Egyptian people being here. So there is nothing more you can do today. Go and eat now. We want to look carefully at these seals again.'

We walked slowly away and everyone began talking excitedly.

'Tariq,' I heard suddenly. 'Could you please wait?'

It was Mr Carter's voice. My friends walked on to the camp, and I went back and looked down the steps.

'Come down,' said Lord Carnarvon. I went down the steps and stood next to him and Mr Carter in front of the tomb door.

'We're going to make a little **hole** in this door and look into the tomb,' said Mr Carter. 'We want you to be with us because your father wants to know everything about our work here. You can **draw** pictures of everything. Do you understand?'

Of course I said 'yes'.

They made a little hole in the door. Carter looked through it with one eye. Lord Carnarvon and I waited. Carter said nothing.

'What can you see?' asked Lord Carnarvon at last.

'Wonderful things!' answered Mr Carter slowly.

Then Lord Carnarvon and I looked. We saw gold and

wake up (*past* **woke up**) to stop sleeping

camp a place where people live in tents for a short time

dream the pictures you see in your head when you are sleeping

hole an opening in something that you can look through or go through

draw (*past* **drew**) to make a picture with a pen or pencil

15

jewels and treasure everywhere behind the door.

'I can see **golden** animals and chairs and—'

'Shh,' said Mr Carter, 'More quietly, please, Tariq! We don't want everyone to hear.'

'Tomorrow we must cover the doors and the steps with sand again,' said Lord Carnarvon. 'But tonight . . .'

He stopped speaking. He and Mr Carter looked at me.

I looked from Lord Carnarvon to Mr Carter. 'Can we go into the tomb tonight?' I asked. 'To have a look?'

'What do you want to do?' asked Lord Carnarvon. 'I think your father would like you to come with us.'

I didn't take long to answer. 'I'm coming,' I said.

We're going into the tomb at midnight with **lights**. We must wait for some hours. When everyone in the camp is sleeping we can go.

November 27th 1922

It took us two hours to make a hole in the door. We worked very quietly, so we couldn't finish by midnight. At 2 a.m. we were ready. Lord Carnarvon went first and then Mr Carter. I went in last, after Lord Carnarvon's daughter. The long room was hot and our lights nearly went out when the air in the tomb moved for the first time in three thousand years. Slowly we began to see strange animals and golden **statues** and chairs. We looked at everything without speaking. All those beautiful things!

I saw a little statue of an Egyptian girl and I remembered the face on it. But from where? Suddenly I knew. It was Anne's face. I remembered my dream. There was something strange happening here. Something between Tutankhamun, Anne and me.

'Look at the two black statues in front of us,' said Mr

golden made of gold

light something you use to see in the dark

statue a figure of a person made of metal or stone

Carter. 'I think they're statues of Tutankhamun. Between them there's a new door. Who wants to go through it with me?'

Lord Carnarvon wanted to go with him, but his daughter and I were afraid. I felt the spirit of Tutankhamun was in the long, hot, dark room with us, and I wanted to get out into the cold night air.

'It's all right,' said Mr Carter. 'You two can wait for us **outside**. But we need your help to make a hole in this new door. It won't take long.'

So we helped them.

It was Anne's face.

After they went through the door, we left the tomb. The **stars** looked down at us and it was very cold. At last the other two came through the door near us. We worked to close the hole carefully.

'What did you see in the second room?' we asked.

'A golden wall,' they answered. 'The body of Tutankhamun is somewhere behind that. This is a wonderful day for all of us.'

By then it was early morning and I went back to my **tent** and slept all day. Now it's evening again, and I'm afraid. But who can I talk to about my feelings?

outside in the open, not in a building

star a far away sun that we see as a little light in the night sky

tent a kind of house made of cloth that you take with you when you move

17

READING CHECK

Correct the mistakes in these sentences.

a   ~~Karim~~ *Tariq* dreams of Anne and Mr Ayrton.

b   The seals on the tomb door are all broken.

c   Tariq can see dead animals through the tomb door.

d   Carter, Carnarvon, Tariq and Evelyn go into the tomb at midnight.

e   There is a door in the tomb between two gold statues of Tutankhamun.

f   Lord Carnarvon and Evelyn go through this door.

g   Tariq and Carter leave the tomb because they are afraid.

WORD WORK

1   Match the words in the snake with the underlined words in the sentences.

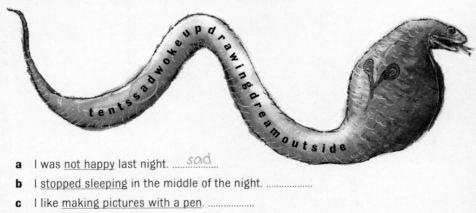

a   I was <u>not happy</u> last night. ....*sad*..........

b   I <u>stopped sleeping</u> in the middle of the night. ....

c   I like <u>making pictures with a pen</u>. ....

d   In summer I like sleeping <u>in the open</u>. ....

e   Carter and his men lived in <u>cloth houses</u> near the valley of the kings. ....

f   People always <u>see pictures in their heads when they sleep</u> at night, but they don't always remember it. ....

2 **Look at the pictures and complete the crossword.**
All the words come from Chapter 3.

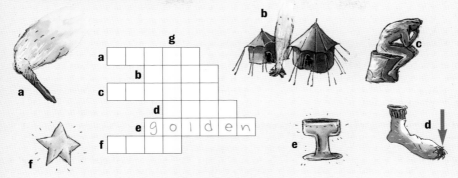

e | g | o | l | d | e | n

3 **Look at the blue squares and write the name of this Egyptian person.**

g _ _ _ _ _ _

GUESS WHAT

What happens in the next chapter? Tick the boxes.

1 Who photographs the things in the tomb?
  a ☐ Mr Carter.
  b ☐ Tariq.
  c ☐ Evelyn.

2 Who feels Tutankhamun is near him?
  a ☐ Mr Carter.
  b ☐ Lord Carnarvon.
  c ☐ Tariq.

3 When do Carter and his men go into the second room in the tomb?
  a ☐ Two months later.
  b ☐ Never.
  c ☐ Twenty years later.

4 What does Tariq dream about?
  a ☐ Anne and Mr Ayrton.
  b ☐ Treasure.
  c ☐ His father in Cairo.

Chapter 4

Every day we find new things

December 22nd 1922

Today, a month after my night visit to the tomb, we opened the tomb door again, this time in front of everybody. Many important Egyptians came to the Valley of the Kings with lots of newspaper men and interested people from all over the world. Many people talked to us, but I said nothing about the golden treasures in the tomb. Only my father knows about them.

When we opened the door in the sunlight, everybody could see the gold and the treasures. First Mr Carter is going to photograph everything we find in the tomb. After the photographs, we can move things and look at them carefully. Then we must write all about each treasure in a book. After that, we must send them to the Museum in Cairo. This work is going to take a long time, but we must be very careful when we move things. Mr Carter picked up a shoe in the tomb today and it broke into little **pieces** in his hands!

January 2nd 1923

Every day we find new things in the first room in the tomb. Today we found some pens and some old Egyptian games. Mr Carter says the **Ancient** Egyptians loved playing games. He says Tutankhamun was happy when he was a little boy. Most of the time, he played with his brothers and sisters in the **palace** gardens. He didn't go to school because he had a teacher in the palace. He couldn't go out of the palace very often because the Egyptian people

pieces when something breaks, it changes from one thing into lots of these

ancient very old

palace a big house where a king lives

thought he was a **god**. They thought all Ancient Egyptian kings and their families were gods. Near the games we found a beautiful golden chair, and there were also many different things to wear. Mr Carter says it took more than 3,000 hours to make only one of his shirts!

Sometimes, when I look at Tutankhamun's things, I feel he's near me. But he died when he was one year older than me. Why? I want to know the answer to that question more than anything.

February 18th 1923

Today, at last, we opened the second room in the tomb. It took us seven weeks to take everything out of the first room. All this time, everyone wanted to go through into the second room, but Mr Carter said: 'No! We must take all the things out of the first room – slowly and carefully – before we do that!'

I know it was difficult for him too, because he knew the second room was the **burial** room.

Lots of people were here again today for the opening of the burial room. It was very hot in the tomb. Mr Carter opened the door between the two black statues and he went in first. When he was in the second room he could see all of the golden wall.

'But it isn't a wall,' he called out to us. 'It's one **side** of a tall, golden **shrine**.'

The shrine nearly filled the second room. It was very difficult to move **around** the shrine because there were treasures on every side of it. On the far side of the burial room is an open door and a third room. This room also has lots of treasures in it. After a short time, Mr Carter asked all our visitors to leave. He said: 'We can't open the shrine

god an important 'person' who never dies, and decides what happens in the world

burial for a dead body to lie in

side a box has six of these

shrine a small, special place for a statue of a god

around all the way round

21

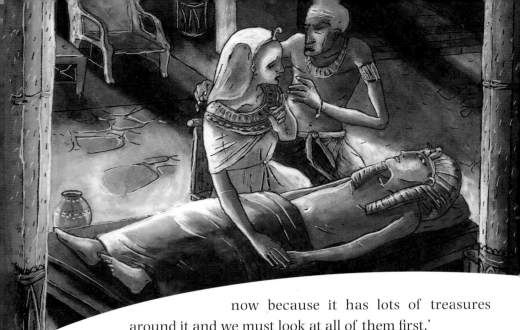

now because it has lots of treasures around it and we must look at all of them first.'

The newspaper men took lots of photos of the shrine and of the treasures and then they left.

'Forget Tutankhamun. He is dying.'

The walls of the burial room are covered with pictures. There are many pictures of Tutankhamun with a young woman. Mr Carter says she is his **queen**, Ankhesenamun. She has a strong, dark face. It makes me think of Anne, the French artist from my dream.

In some of the pictures, Ankhesenamun is giving Tutankhamun flowers, and he is smiling at her. They look very happy. Mr Carter thinks they *were* very happy when they married. Am I going to be happy when I marry? I'd like to marry Anne. But where is she now? Back in France? Or here in Egypt in a museum somewhere, looking at Ancient Egyptian jewels and statues?

After Tutankhamun died, Mr Carter says, the next king of Egypt was Lord Ay, a man twenty years older than Tutankhamun. When Mr Carter told me about this, I remembered my bad dream of Anne and the old Egyptian

queen the wife of a king

22

mummy in the sands of the desert. And I remembered the time when her eye bracelet fell in the sand.

After work today I slept and had another dream. This time I saw Anne wearing a white Egyptian dress. She had Egyptian jewels in her hair and Egyptian bracelets on her arms. We were in a room in an old Egyptian palace. I **lay** with my eyes open on an old Egyptian bed and she sat next to the bed on an old Egyptian chair.

'Tutankhamun,' she said, holding my hand, 'Lord Ay is watching me all the time now, and I am afraid.'

I wanted to say, 'My name's Tariq', but I couldn't speak.

'What is going to happen to me when you die?' she asked.

Again I could say nothing.

'First our two children, and now you. People say Lord Ay killed them. And they say he's killing you, too, with **poison** because he wants to marry me and be king of Egypt.'

Suddenly a man came quietly into the room behind her. He wore a white Ancient Egyptian skirt, but he had the face of Anne's teacher, Mr Ayrton! I wanted to tell Anne to look behind her, but I couldn't open my mouth. The man came to her and put his hand on her arm.

'Ankhesenamun,' he said, smiling coldly. 'Forget Tutankhamun. He is dying. You must take a new husband now. Are you ready to be my wife?'

I woke up suddenly, crying 'Anne! No! Don't do it!'

Karim sleeps in the tent next to me, and he woke up when he heard my voice.

'What's the matter, Tariq?' he said. 'It's three o'clock in the morning! Are you crazy?'

Am I crazy? Why am I having these dreams? I don't understand them. Are they telling me to stop working for Mr Carter and to leave the Valley of the Kings?

lie (*past* **lay**) to have all of your body on a bed

poison something that kills people when they eat or drink it

READING CHECK

Correct seven more mistakes in this summary of Chapter 4.

opening
Many important people come to see the ~~closing~~ of Tutankhamun's tomb. Mr Carter is
going to draw and write about all the things in the tomb before sending them to the
Museum in London. Carter and his men find pens, games, shirts and a beautiful golden
bed in the first room of the tomb. After seven days of hard work there are no more things
in it. Then Carter and his men can go through into the second room. This room has
pictures of King Tutankhamun and his mother, Ankhesenamun, on its walls. After work
Tariq sleeps, and he has a dream about being Lord Ay. He sees Ankhesenamun in his
sleep. She has the face of the German artist, Anne.

WORD WORK

Use the words in the picture to complete the sentences on page 25.

Ancient
around
burial
god
lie
palaces

pieces
poison
queen
shrine
side

a He broke the bread into very small p i e c e s for the birds.

b I like reading about _ _ _ _ _ _ _ Egypt – about Tutankhamun and Nefertiti and their times.

c Ra was the Egyptian _ _ _ of the sun. They thought he moved the sun through the sky on his ship.

d Egyptian kings didn't live in small houses, they lived in very big _ _ _ _ _ _ _ _ .

e Cleopatra was _ _ _ _ _ of Egypt in Julius Caesar's time.

f Would you like to _ _ _ on this bed and sleep?

g Don't drink that! It's got _ _ _ _ _ _ in it!

h There was a statue of Hathor in a golden _ _ _ _ _ _ .

i The dead king lay in one room of the tomb – the _ _ _ _ _ _ room.

j Carter and Lord Carnarvon walked _ _ _ _ _ _ the tomb, looking at everything.

k Each _ _ _ _ of the box had a different picture on it.

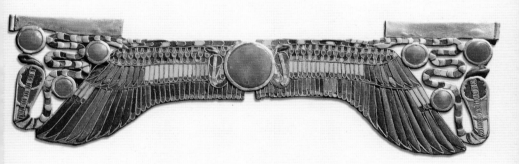

GUESS WHAT

What happens in the next chapter? Tick the boxes.	Yes	Perhaps	No
a Tariq goes to England.	☐	☐	☐
b Lord Carnarvon dies.	☐	☐	☐
c Carter dies.	☐	☐	☐
d Carter finds the bodies of Tutankhamun's children.	☐	☐	☐
e Lord Carnarvon's daughter dies.	☐	☐	☐
f All the lights in Cairo go out.	☐	☐	☐

Chapter 5

Tutankhamun's mummy is killing people

March 15th 1923

We had some bad news today. Lord Carnarvon is very ill. Mr Carter says it's because of the poison from a bad **mosquito bite**. Mosquitoes can be **dangerous** in Egypt. Some people are saying that he's ill because the spirit of Tutankhamun is angry. In the newspapers, a woman called Maria Corelli says that he's going to die because Tutankhamun is angry. Some people say that all of us here are going to die soon because we opened the tomb. So nobody is sleeping easily in their tents tonight. We're all thinking about the spirit of Tutankhamun. Is he angry with us? And why am I dreaming about that French girl, the artist, Anne? Where is she now? I'm **sure** we're going to meet again. But where?

April 6th 1923

Lord Carnarvon is dead. I am sorry because I liked him and his daughter, Evelyn. The newspapers say that all the lights in Cairo went out when he died. The city was dark for many hours. Mr Carter told us that Lord Carnarvon's dog died in England on that night too. Mr Carter only laughs at the things in the newspapers. He's not afraid of anything. But he's sorry too: Lord Carnarvon was a good friend.

May 29th 1923

People are talking about Lord Carnarvon dying. They are saying that we were wrong to go into a dead man's tomb. But Mr Carter doesn't listen to anybody. He wants to open

mosquito a small insect that drinks people's and animals' blood

bite where a mosquito takes blood from someone

dangerous something that could kill you

sure when you feel something is true

the shrine in the burial room soon and find the body of Tutankhamun. It's going to take us all summer to finish our work on the things in the burial room and the treasure room, but what happens then? Are we all going to die after finding the body of the boy-king?

October 3rd 1923

A week ago we sent the last treasure from the first room to the museum. My father has everything now. In his last letter, he told me they are looking for more workers at the museum in Cairo. My father has a lot of work to do there now because the museum has lots of visitors every week. Everyone wants to see Tutankhamun's beautiful things.

Mr Carter thinks we can open the shrine some time in the winter, perhaps in December.

December 12th 1923

Today we opened the shrine. In it there was a second golden shrine. We must open this very carefully!

January 20th 1924

There are three golden shrines! After opening all three of them, we found a stone **sarcophagus**. How much more must we open before we find Tutankhamun?

November 12th 1924

When we opened the sarcophagus we found a golden **coffin**, with two more golden coffins inside it. On each we saw a beautiful golden face – the face of Tutankhamun. I know his face well now from all the pictures on the walls of the tomb. On the last coffin, his head is blue and gold, and he has a golden snake and a bird's head over his big, dark

sarcophagus a stone box that you put a dead person's body in

coffin a wooden or metal box that you put a dead person's body in

eyes. These mean he was king of the North and the South of Egypt, Mr Carter says.

Today, at last, we found the mummy of Tutankhamun. It is only a young boy's body inside all that gold and treasure. Around the mummy were 143 jewels of all colours: red, green, white and blue. There were also some blue flowers. I'm sure his beautiful queen Ankhesenamun put them there. When we found the body, there were lots of people in the room and it was very hot, but I felt cold and afraid. Mr Carter was very excited. But I could only hear a little voice in my head. The voice said to me it was wrong to be there. I left the tomb and ran outside into the warm sun. But I felt cold out there, too.

In the evening, Mr Carter came to my tent.

'Why did you suddenly leave us, Tariq?' he asked.

I told him that I felt afraid of Tutankhamun's spirit.

'You're tired,' he said. 'You need a holiday. Why don't you visit your father for one or two weeks? I know he'd like to see you. You can help him in the museum.'

'Thank you, Mr Carter,' I answered.

'And remember, Tutankhamun died three thousand years ago. He can't be angry with anybody any more.'

'Perhaps not,' I said, but I wasn't sure.

So tomorrow morning I'm going back to Cairo! All my things are ready in my bag and my diary's coming with me too. I'm going to be far away when the doctor comes to cut up Tutankhamun's body. I don't want to see that. I hope my father understands.

I'm looking at the stars now. I must say goodbye to my best friends in the desert.

January 14th 1925: Cairo

I'm not going back to the camp. My father and I spoke about it today. All over the world, people are saying Tutankhamun's mummy is killing people. And my friend Karim died last week at the camp. How did he die? I don't know, but I know everybody's going to say Tutankhamun's angry spirit killed him. Mr Carter still isn't afraid, but he's the only one now. My father doesn't believe in 'the **curse** of the mummy', but he wants me to stay with him and help him in Cairo in the museum.

Last week Mr Carter found more coffins and the mummies of two little children. He thinks they are Tutankhamun's children. They died before they were born. I feel sorry for the boy-king and his beautiful young queen. We're going to look after all his things very carefully here in Cairo. Then perhaps he isn't going to get angry with me or my father.

curse to make something bad happen to someone by saying that it is going to happen

29

READING CHECK

1 Are these sentences true or false? Tick the boxes.

		True	False
a	Some people think Tutankhamun is angry with Mr Carter.	☑	☐
b	They say Tutankhamun wants to kill Carter and his men.	☐	☐
c	Tariq is happy when Lord Carnarvon dies.	☐	☐
d	Mr Carter is very excited when he opens the mummy.	☐	☐
e	Tariq feels happy about opening the mummy.	☐	☐
f	Carter's father writes to him.	☐	☐
g	Tariq goes to work in England.	☐	☐

2 Put the correct letters at the end of each sentence:
HC **(Howard Carter),** *LC* **(Lord Carnarvon), or** *T* **(Tariq).**

a He becomes ill. ..*LC*....

b He thinks of the French girl, Anne. ....

c His dog dies. ....

d He laughs at the things in the newspapers. ....

e He wants to go on working in Tutankhamun's tomb. ....

f He hears a voice in his head. ....

g He doesn't think Tutankhamun is angry with anyone. ....

WORD WORK

Find words in the puzzle and complete the sentences on page 31.

bi	cu	sar	ous	ag
rse	dan	te	in	su
~~qui~~	coph	cof	us	~~to~~
ger	re	~~mos~~	fin	side

30

a I can hear a mosquito flying around the bedroom and I can't get to sleep.

b There's a snake .... on his foot. Perhaps that killed him.

c It's very .... to go across the desert without taking any water with you.

d There's picture writing over the door to the tomb. I think it's a .... and it says we are all going to die.

e Are you .... this is Tutankhamun's tomb? I don't think it is.

f The dead king's body lay in a gold .... and that was in a big stone ....

g Is there anything in that box? No, there's nothing .... it.

GUESS WHAT

The next chapter is seven years later. What happens? Tick the boxes.

a Mr Carter . . .
  1 ☐ is suddenly ill and dies.
  2 ☐ finishes his work in Tutankhamun's tomb.
  3 ☐ goes crazy.

b Tariq . . .
  1 ☐ meets the French artist Anne again.
  2 ☐ never sees the French artist Anne again.
  3 ☐ reads about the French Artist Anne in the newspaper.

c Tariq's father . . .
  1 ☐ doesn't like Anne.
  2 ☐ thinks Anne is bad for his son.
  3 ☐ thinks Anne is a good artist.

d Anne and Tariq . . .
  1 ☐ learn to say goodbye to the past.
  2 ☐ die in a car accident.
  3 ☐ marry.

Chapter 6

The end of a wonderful time

February 13th 1932

It's time for me to finish my diary now. I stopped writing it seven years ago, but the story of Tutankhamun's tomb didn't finish then. For seven more years Mr Carter and his workers stayed in the Valley of the Kings. They found a small fourth room in the tomb. There was **food** and drink there. (Would anyone like some 3,000-year-old bread?) There were also thirty bottles of **wine**! There were many more beautiful treasures in the fourth room too. We have them all in the museum here in Cairo now. I'm happy to say no more workers died at the camp and Mr Carter is still alive and very well.

The last treasure arrived at the museum three weeks ago and then Mr Carter at last left the Valley of the Kings. He's coming to our house tonight, and we're all going out to have dinner at the best restaurant in Cairo.

'It's the end of a wonderful time,' my father says. 'We're going to have an evening to remember.'

Four of us are going to the restaurant: Mr Carter, my father, the French artist Anne, and me. I met Anne again at the museum a year ago. She came to make some pictures of Tutankhamun's treasures. When she arrived at the museum, I remembered her at once and she remembered me. So it was easy to begin to talk.

'And what happened to your old teacher, Mr Ayrton?' I asked soon after we met.

'Oh, him!' said Anne and she laughed, 'What a bad man he was!'

food you eat this

wine a red or white drink; when you drink a lot you feel happy and sleepy

'What do you mean?' I asked.

'He wasn't a good teacher. He was a tomb thief, only interested in getting ancient Egyptian treasures.'

I looked at the Egyptian eye bracelet on her arm. Anne's eyes met my eyes.

'Yes. He liked beautiful things, and in the end, I think I was only one more beautiful thing for him to look at. So I left him. I'm much happier now. I feel free without Mr Ayrton, without his eyes watching me all the time.'

Anne and I worked in one of my father's offices at the museum for some weeks and in that time we talked about many things – often about Tutankhamun. Anne feels the boy-king is her friend. And I feel I understand him very well, too.

We talked about many things.

We all had a wonderful time last night.

My father likes Anne. He says she's a very good artist, and she loves Egypt – the ancient country and the new country, too. She says she would like to live here always. Would she like to marry an Egyptian man? I'm not sure. But I think I'm going to ask her one day soon.

A taxi is stopping outside our door. It's Anne and Mr Carter. I must go downstairs and meet them.

February 14th 1932

We all had a wonderful time last night. The food and wine were very good and everybody talked and laughed a lot in the restaurant. Mr Carter looks very happy and not much older than seven years ago. It was nice to see him again.

Nobody could think that Tutankhamun's spirit is angry with him. Mr Carter and I talked more about Karim. Some people are saying there were dangerous **bacteria** inside the tomb and these killed my friend. But why only Karim? Other people say the ancient Egyptians put poison in the tombs to kill tomb thieves. Mr Carter thinks these stories are wrong. He says there was nothing strange about it. One day Karim got dangerously ill and died before the doctor could get to the camp.

My father told Mr Carter about the new stories in the English newspapers. People in England are now afraid of having mummies and ancient Egyptian treasures in their houses. They're sending them all to the British Museum. And the Museum is going to need a new room to keep all these things in. Some people think that the great *Titanic* accident happened because the ship had an Egyptian mummy on it. A museum in New York wanted the mummy for its Egyptian rooms, but when the *Titanic* went down in the Atlantic, the mummy went down with the ship.

After dinner my father asked Mr Carter, 'Do you want to go and see *The Mummy?*' It's a new film here in Cairo and everybody loves it. Boris Karloff is the mummy. He's a very famous **film star** in Cairo these days.

Mr Carter laughed again and said 'Why not?' So he went to the cinema with my father.

But Anne and I didn't want to go with them. We can't laugh about the curse of the mummy. I think the spirit of Tutankhamun doesn't do anything bad to Mr Carter because he isn't a tomb thief. He found Tutankhamun's treasure, but he's leaving it here in Egypt. With my father's help the Tutankhamun rooms in the Cairo museum are

bacteria these small things can make you ill

film star you see this famous person in a film

now beautiful. So Tutankhamun isn't angry with my father or with Mr Carter. But I'm not sure about Lord Carnarvon or my friend Karim. Why did they die? And what about me and Anne?

Anne and I walked slowly back to her hotel from the restaurant. The stars over Cairo were wonderful that night and I told her how the stars were my friends in the desert.

'Let's go to the museum,' she said suddenly. 'You've got your **key**, haven't you?'

'Yes, of course,' I answered. 'I always have it with me.'

We went there at once and, with my key, I opened the museum door and we went into Tutankhamun's rooms. We looked at one of the golden shrines there. On it there's a picture of Tutankhamun and his queen Ankhesenamun at a table. She's putting some wine into his glass. Some women are playing **music** for them. It's wonderful to think this all happened thousands of years ago!

'I think they were happy for a time,' Anne said, 'before Lord Ay came along, before their children died, and before Tutankhamun died. And perhaps they can be happy again now. Who knows?'

She took my hand.

'I want to leave my bracelet here, Tariq,' she said. 'For Tutankhamun and Ankhesenamun. I don't need it now, you see. Now I have you. So I can close the door on Mr Ayrton, and on Lord Ay.' She took the Egyptian eye bracelet from her arm and put it down in front of the golden shrine. When she put the bracelet down, I thought I could hear far away music, and some strange and beautiful singing coming from somewhere. In my head I closed the door on Lord Carnarvon, on my friend Karim, and on Tutankhamun's curse, and I felt happy.

key you can close or open a door with this

music singing or playing instruments

Then Anne and I left the museum, arm in arm.

She was free of Mr Ayrton and I was free of the mummy's curse at last. I smiled at Anne and she smiled at me. We walked slowly back to her hotel and said goodbye at the door.

'See you tomorrow morning,' said Anne looking at me, with stars in her eyes.

'Yes, see you tomorrow morning,' I answered, and I walked back home, happy and excited, dreaming of asking Anne to marry me.

'I want to leave my bracelet here.'

READING CHECK

Match the first and second parts of these sentences.

a   Mr Carter and his men find . . .

b   Anne comes . . .

c   Mr Ayrton thinks . . .

d   Anne leaves . . .

e   Tariq and his father are
going . . .

f   Mr Carter doesn't think . . .

g   Tariq's father and Carter go . . .

h   Tariq and Anne . . .

i   Anne leaves her Egyptian eye
bracelet . . .

j   Tariq wants to ask Anne . . .

1   to Cairo museum to draw Tutankhamun's
treasures.

2   Mr Ayrton and feels free now.

3   to the cinema after dinner.

4   a fourth room in Tutankhamun's tomb.

5   Anne is beautiful.

6   to a restaurant with Anne and Mr Carter.

7   in the Tutankhamun rooms of the
museum.

8   there is a curse on Tutankhamun's tomb.

9   to marry him.

10   walk to the museum.

WORD WORK

**Use the words in the Egyptian mummy
to complete the sentences.**

a   'When do you like listening to .....music.?'
'When I am working in my room.'

b   'Where's the .... to this door?'
'I don't know. Can't you open the door without it?'

c   'Which .... do you like the best?'
'Julia Roberts.'

d   This kitchen is very dirty. And a dirty kitchen has
.... everywhere and that can make you very ill.

wine

bacteria

film star

key

food

music

e 'Would you like some ....?'
'No thanks. I'm not hungry.'

f 'I'd like some .... to drink.'
'Red or white?'

GUESS WHAT

What happens after the story ends? Choose from these ideas or add your own.

a ☐ Howard Carter dies suddenly.

b ☐ Howard Carter lives to be an old man.

c ☐ Tariq and Anne get married.

d ☐ Mr Ayrton comes angrily to take Anne from Tariq.

e ☐ The mummy of Tutankhamun really starts killing people.

f ☐ ....

g ☐ ....

h ☐ ....

PROJECT A

Anne's Diary

1 Read this page from Anne's diary. Answer the questions.

a What does she think of Egypt?
b What does she feel and why?
c What does she want to do next year?
d Where did she go in the morning?
e What is she doing these days?
f Who did she meet?
g What did he do?
h What does she think about this?
i What must she do?

September 12th 1922

Egypt is golden, hot and wonderful! I'm sad because we're here for only two weeks. I want to come back next year and stay here for longer. I'm drawing lots of pictures these days. In the morning I went to the

Valley of the Kings. I met a young Egyptian man in the Valley. He helped me to find my Egyptian bracelet when it fell into the sand. I think it was nice of him to help but I don't think Mr Ayrton was very happy about it. I must be careful.

2 **Anne goes back to France. Write a page from her diary. Use these words to complete the sentences.**

January 14th 1923

France is ....

I'm not very happy because ....

....

I want to go ....

I'm not drawing ....

This morning, I ....

I met ....

but he didn't ....

I think it was ....

I must leave ....

back to Egypt!

much these days.

went to Art School.

crazy of me to like him.

cold, dark and strange.

Paris soon.

Mr Ayrton in his office,

it's wintertime here.

speak to me.

3 **Write a different page from Anne's diary.**

PROJECT B

A box of your things

1 **Howard Carter found many things in Tutankhamun's tomb. These things give us a good picture of ancient Egyptian times. Match the pictures with the sentences.**

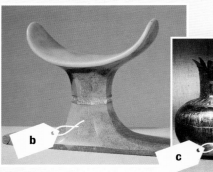

1 ☐ We think King Tutankhamun liked eating fruit.

2 ☐ We think he liked drinking wine.

3 ☐ We think he played this game.

4 ☐ We know he wore these in his ears.

5 ☐ We think he used this chair when he was a child.

6 ☐ We know he put his head on this when he went to bed at night.

2 **Think of people in 3010 finding things from today.**
Can you match the pictures with the sentences?

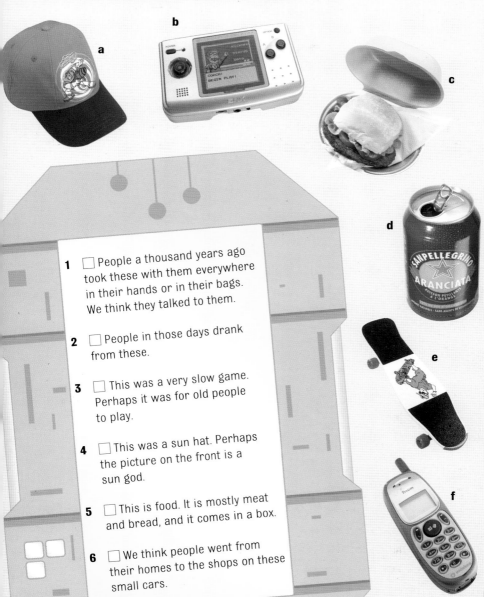

a

b

c

d

e

f

1 ☐ People a thousand years ago took these with them everywhere in their hands or in their bags. We think they talked to them.

2 ☐ People in those days drank from these.

3 ☐ This was a very slow game. Perhaps it was for old people to play.

4 ☐ This was a sun hat. Perhaps the picture on the front is a sun god.

5 ☐ This is food. It is mostly meat and bread, and it comes in a box.

6 ☐ We think people went from their homes to the shops on these small cars.

3 You want to give people thousands of years from now a picture of your life today. What twelve things can you put in a box one metre by one metre by one metre?

CHECKLIST

Things to wear:

Games to play:

Things to eat:

Things to drink:

Things to use in your free time:

Things from your room or house:

4 Now imagine you are someone from 3010 and write about the things in your box.

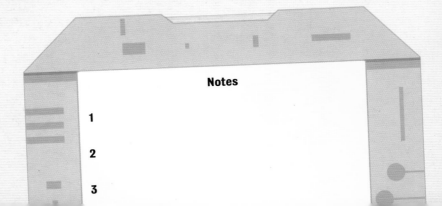

Notes

1

2

3